AF454172

Kisses, Not Done Yet

Mamun Ashraphi

Clever Fox
PUBLISHING

Chennai • Bangalore

CLEVER FOX PUBLISHING
Chennai, India

Published by CLEVER FOX PUBLISHING 2023
Copyright © Mamun Ashraphi 2023

All Rights Reserved.
ISBN: 978-93-56482-82-1

Dedicated to

My most respected late parents;
Two immortal souls
Daulatur Rahman Ashraphi
And
Momotaj Begum
Those who
taught:
Truth and justice are life;
Lies and covetousness are sins;
Sin causes the death of humanity and the soul;
So accept the truth and reject sin.

CONTENTS

PROLOGUE

Poetry is a noble art because it beautifies and purifies the human soul. So, in my opinion, poetry is exclusively for those who value beauty and intelligence. Poetry is for those who are profoundly artistic, curious, and creative.

Poetry is arguably the most admired and creative, aesthetic art form among all evidence of creativity in the world. Poetry has thus been recognized as a pioneering art form and the most aesthetically pleasing discipline of creative expression for thousands of years.

To write aesthetic poetry, the thirty-three poetries in this collection were composed over a lengthy period of approximately three years (2018-2021). The reason was that thirty years ago, during theesteemed period of my transition from adolescence to youth, the brain and the heart were torn apart when poetry flowed through me, like a cyclone; at that time, when poetry used to stir wretchedness in the blood; at that time, when the invigorating and treacherous nature of first love resonated in the heart every moment. Even then, I had no idea what poetry was until the pen created each of my favorite poetries. And the moment I realized what poetry is, the pen abruptly stopped moving. I started to grasp that the first step in actually writingpoetry is to study poetry to comprehend what poetry is, and then to subsequently certify myself as a poet.

Consequently, it may be said that I have studied, tried to qualify myself to write poetry and sought to understand poetry for over three long decades. I even had to observe and think for more than twelve years before I could write some of the poetry.

Even though some or all of the poetries in this book may be a waste of paper and fail the poetic quality test, these are the prized result of my extensive artistic reflection and observation. These poetries have grown so precious to me, and what makes them even more significant is that practically all of them have successfully passed many tests regarding their subject matter and mode of expression to be published in its current format. It can be argued that these poetries represent my beliefs and observations on people, nature, the country, politics, society, religion, love, lust, the body, etc., as well as my philosophy.

During the renaissance of modern Bengali poetry - the poets of that era and especially the five main poets who enriched Bengali poetry with their thought, philosophy, and observation have discarded some of my favorite words. In my view, Bengali poetry has lost a lot of its elegance. That's because, in modern social, political, and literary contexts, I believe those word still have equal weight and significance. Additionally, it appears that some words have greater significance than ever before and are capable of causing more suffering. I have thus attempted to include them into my songs and poetries, out of love and passion for these forgotten words, and I believe that the reader and time will decide their fates; only a select few poets will not be able to foretell its future.

Similar to how a thousand-year-old civilization grew to where it is today, poetry has also progressed over time.

Most of the poetry that was part of the ancient Bengali literature that has been recovered is called "Charyapad," and it is essentially a collection of mystical poetries and songs of realization. It is among the oldest pieces of Bengali poetry. Between the eighth and twelfth centuries AD is thought to have seen the composition of "Charyapad."

As a result, poetry had a long journey to its current state, through several changes and experimentation throughout history. Poetry is improved, enriched, and evolved via experimentation and evolution, it also takes on the form of today's modern poetry as a result. Poetry has been evolving over time and will continue to do so. The same is true of poetry written in all other languages as well as Bengali.

Additionally, poetry only depicts the present. Poetry addresses topics such as philosophy, politics, religion, love, betrayal, beauty, the Earth and the universe, as well as the past, present, and even future civilizations. Poetry touches on every topic under the sun. Poetry is a timeless and comprehensive art form, not just something of the present. Perhaps no other art form has had such widespread human interaction as poetry, with its many poets and readers.

As a result of poetry's ability to arouse a person's sense of beauty and need for information, they become immediately enamored by it. That notion suggests that poetry has magical qualities. Poetry expresses the innermost sensations of the human heart, which is why people turn solely to poetry in times of joy and sorrow.

All poets compose poetries on various topics, though others choose to write about a specific one. Because of this, certain poets are referred to be "poets of love", while others are "poets of rebellion" or "poets of nature".

Among many other subjects, love, the organ, and nature predominate in early Bengali and most other languages' poetry. These few topics have been chosen up until now as the major aspects of poets' writings and thoughts, and poets have attempted to explain and arrange these topics in poetry in a very beautiful way. The body is kept as silent and sideways as possible in Bengali poetry, where nature and love are represented and portrayed as lovely, majestic, and sacred.

Except for a few writers, the body is not viewed as being particularly significant in modern Bengali poetry. And while sexuality is carefully avoided, the body is given prominence. However, I believe that lust and love are linked and that there is no justifiable reason to ignore them in a man-woman relationship. Instead, sexuality is a wonderful beauty that is frequently admired by many people, but while this happiness is present, it is mercilessly contained within a privacy fence. Sexuality is no less wonderful and lovely than love, in fact, it is forever linkedto it.

The significance, greatness, and beauty of *Kama* in the lives of people are not encas Kisses, Not Done Yet ed in a wall of secrecy in our Pak-India subcontinent, even though the western way of life, literature and culture are kept out. Even more than what is disclosed in cave arts and temple wall murals are concealed in poetry. The walls of temples in India's Ajanta, Konark, Ellora, and especially Khajuraho bear clear testimony to it.

So, since the beauty, importance, and magnificence of *Kama*are discussed in ancient books, why *Kama* is overlooked in current Bengali poetries, this topic stands as a significant query to me. What role does employment play in our social and personal lives, then? There cannot be a justification for this! While there is love between a man and a woman, lust cannot be denied because the two are intertwined. Poetry thus catches the individual, society, and time; it also contains all the following thoughts and ideas of humans, so there should always be new poetry being produced. However, I believe it is important to value lust as a subject of modern poetry as much as love, and modern poets should play a more daring role in their poetry by using descriptions of the hidden beauty of romance. It is possible to research why this topic is being neglected in modern Bengali poetry.

Along with love, this hitherto disregarded body and desire have taken on more significance in my poetry. My poetry's main theme is the attraction of a man and a woman's love and bodies, as well as their hidden beauty and appeal to our lives and psyches. I want to investigate whether poetry actually appeals to us and whether readers will embrace my poetries on love and the body. I wanted to test whether renouncing lust could lead to any fulfillment in our lives and poetries.

The above-mentioned ways in which *Kama* was glorified and represented in India throughout the ninth century are still evident in our daily lives, yet oddly and puzzlingly, poetry does not reflect them. Life and poetry are now devoid of desire, which is unimaginable! Therefore, I believe that by excluding it from modern Bengali poetry, a significant component of human life has been unjustifiably left out. This has left Bengali poetry with a sense of incompleteness, and in the future, it may also call into question historical understanding.

Many people think it's inappropriate to employ *Kama* in poetry. Obscenity has no limits and cannot be restricted, despite the fact that it can be broadly defined. Lust is never inappropriate. If so, why do we treasure this animosity in our bodies and emotions, and why are we implementing it in our daily life?

Eroticism or descriptions of sexual activity may seem obscene to one person but not to another. Therefore, I reject all swearing in poetry. Perspective plays a role in profanity. Only a poet understands how to offer his poetry to the reader and how much sexual beauty to combine there, thus it must be assumed that any profanity in poetry is used because it is required or unavoidable for the beauty of the poetry. The reader will determine how much to accept or reject. The reader's acceptance is key to the poetry and the poet's success.

My point is that poetry depicts people's thoughts and lives, thus even if poetryis considered vulgar by some readers, it may still be considered acceptable by literary standards or other readers. How much of a necessity or function does the alleged vulgarity in poetry actually serve? Maybe time and the public will provide an answer.

Mamun Ashraphi,
Shantinagar, Dhaka, Bangladesh
E-mail: ceo@amazing-cso.com
January 2022

I WANT TO SAY SOMETHING

I adore reading poetry. One day, I was handed a book by a new poet. I opened the book and began reading. To immerse oneself in the poetry and keep them for later reading, I believe that one should read no more than one or two poetries at a time. However, the thirty-three poetries in this collection, I read through in a single sitting. I was quite taken aback. Warum, how? I questioned after finishing the book. The reason seems to be that after reading the first two poetries, I thought they would be superior if they were written in English. And because its content is the major factor.

The poet has expressed all of these topics in his poetries with utmost honesty, including *kama*, sex, the feminine body, and love. In old Bengali literature, it was common to express these ideas openly, but in contemporary literature, these sentiments are conveyed through subterfuge. However, the poet Mamur Ashraphi in his book *Asamamto Chumban* (Unfinished Kiss) has distinctly expressed his feelings in the tone of nostalgia in the poetry.

Nirmalendu Guna, a major poet of our country, Bangladesh, wrote in one of his books, "Sex-passion, anger, greed, infatuation, vanity and envy. In the Bengali dictionary, these six inherent is considered as mischief. My opinion on the other five-inherent is lexicographic, but I cannot think of *Kama* as a vice." In his book, he reveals the many instincts of *Kama* and the female body in the context of poetry. At one place the poet writes, "But I, the ghost of polygamy alone / the poet of one desire, do not believe so. / I know that life is polygamous, by nature, by intuition."It is true that the poet has a 'confession of a polygamist' with extraordinary enthusiasm, but I think I could not accept the poet's lust.

All of Mr. NirmalenduGuna's "Kamkanan" poetries include this lust-sickness. I think there is a very thin line between being modest and crossing it. Many well-known poets, including many contemporary poets, have images of this lust-sickness in their work. "The most beautiful girl will drag all night with both hands / Suck the penis of the spoiled man; On lust's filthy thighs / There shall be goddesses of the paragon of beauty," Humayun Azad penned in one of his poetries. That's correct—views are not irrational. But there was another way to say it. I don't believe that would have been at all difficult for a learned man like Humayun Azad.

As beautifully at ease Sunil Gangopadhyay wrote in one of his poetries, "If you had promised you would teach careless intercourse – / Breast washed with dew, vagina like a soft moonlight / Hair like fresh grasses, slightly dark-brown / If you had promised you would teach careless intercourse". Here his imagery or choice of words are polite and pretty enough. No exaggeration. If we talk about modern poets writing in English, we can talk about many who write about sex and intercourse in their poetries, but not beyond the border of modesty. Louise Gluck can serve as an example. In a poetry, she composed, "Because I wanted to be burned, stamped, / to have something in the end- / I drew the gown over my head; / a red flush covered my face and shoulders. / It will run its course, the course of fire, / setting a cold coin on the forehead, between the eyes."

From WILLIAM SHAKESPEARE, all the way to Allen Ginsberg, many poets have talked about sex in their poetries.

Metamorphoses by the Roman poet Ovid may be considered the first sexual poetry ever written.

A character in Federico Garca Lorca's play *Blood Wedding* says something that is quite true: "To burn with desire and keep quiet about it is the greatest punishment we can bring on ourselves. What good was pride to me—and not seeing you and letting you lie awake at night after night? No good! It only served to bring the fire down on me! You think that time heals and walls hide things, but it isn't true, it isn't true! When things get that deep inside you there isn't anybody can change them." There is only one justification for saying this much: Mamur Ashraphi, a poet who shies away from vulgarity, has described his feelings and thoughts in his poetry collection *Asamamto Chumban*. The book begins with a lengthy apology from Mr. Ashraphi. He willingly provided information on the poetry he writes and how it came to be poetries. Although he has long been a poet, he has never bothered to have it published.

When I later met Mr. Ashraphi, I learned that he shares my opinion that these should be conducted in English. I was given authorization and accountability for the translation. I've already spoken about the poetries' content. The poetries will serve as memories for the middle-aged while serving as an oracle for the young.

I gave it some thought since, if the poetries' points of inspiration could be communicated in English, the book might find a wider audience of readers throughout the world, because the poetries' ideas are universal and likely to hold the top spot among all emotions.

Ashraf ul Alam Shikder
Bashaboo, Dhaka, Bangladesh
December 2022

The Love

I'vemislaideverything, but still not your memories

So many Golden days and moonlit nights have passed away?

Amid the Monsoon clouds, at the fog of Winters, merely for you – those of my melodies

still awakes in my soul as a star there.

At the first spark of a glimpse, the forest caughtfire

Oh, my sweetheart, you agile lady with coquetry in eyes

You did seize the heart of mine unnoticed, I had lost all pleasure and aspire

You, honeybee, had come to my garth of love, and to agonize.

So even now, I am looking for just you in every town and harbor.

Thus, my eyes never close, at whatever time of the night or day.

My vigilant heart is listening to the melody of the air

Many cruel nights I had spent wandering on the streets,
and bay.

While I roamed from one country to another in Asia,
America, or Europe,

At the crystalline lakes, in the lap of evergreens beneath the
shadow of the mountain

Again and again, only one face floated in the heart with a
hope

And despite my hundreds of efforts, I couldn't forget her
even

Although the burning of the first touch of the first love is
extinguished

It doesn't go out but keeps me scorched day after day.

She would burn down me to ashes with herself, bit by bit

The more she burns, the more omnivorous she became as a
dead lay!

Body and Love

Oh, dear, that's not only body, I want your heart too;

The heart resides in the body

And therein lies love

To realize the fact you have expended

A lifetime in its entirety

To protect the corpse from the clasp of *Kama*

You have lost the sweet feelings of love

And you have lost a few vivid agonies

Why is the body burning today due to the pain of the loss?

Heart is burning too, Love is not there

No loving pleasures and pains

Alas! Whether current existence is a waste!

Divulge to me what else is more there in you!

Except for a pair of lips and breasts one pair and

The divinity of a half-cut apple!

And how long does it take you to understand?

Without sex, a body is nothing.

The body is essential for lust and love to survive;

Only sex does not quench thirst; and no one has ever been satisfied;

See, love is awakened beyond the boundaries of sex,

But love is more expensive than the body!

It is Known as the Human Life

I experienced that twilight you

In a tight hug of mine

Inexpressible delight of being beside,

While extending that dusk

All of a sudden, I felt

Lengthy sixty seconds had passed,

Within a few moments!

You had uttered, love means a distance

And not to be approached closer anyways;

Or staying afar even when nearby

Where the awe of missing stays ibid every moment

But cuddling is a lust

And lust means the destruction of affection!

As far as I'm aware,

Love resides in the heart.

And there all over the physique

Is only venery and wantonness

The human body is dominated by greed.

According to the label on the package of love

Servitude to rapacity,

However, it is known as the Human Life

I Won't Ever Go Anywhere From You

I won't ever go anywhere from you

Retain this hand; hold this tiny finger of mine;

Don't ever let the grasp go loose

I had lost my heart long before

In your tender warmth,

Since then,it has merged in

Blue-sky and white clouds

In your deepest green, delighting forest

In your beautiful olivaceous;

And since then, I -

Were only with you, my darling,

My leafyBengali;

I am still within you

Preoccupied with the smell of your soil

One day I will get to the bottom of your land;

Telling you the truth and just the truth

I would never

Leave you anywhere

This isn't my promise

This is my assured future.

Love is Nothing But a Flame

Love is nothing but a flame

Spring of the inferno

It never ends in detachment

The burning of that fire

Will there in your whole life

Lives as an attachment.

Never it burns thou body,

That the spring of the fire

It only anneals your spirit

With all the secret weapons

It kills inside you to ashes

Merciless is its perception

After These Thirty-three Years

Keep thee pair of hands on mine, dear

After thirty-three years on this eve today

The first love poetry ever I written

Do you still remember, it may.

From this cloudy afternoon to monsoon evening

As if rain is falling from my eyes, to say

In the Delusion of the torrential rain

Only you are remembered, my fay!

My life is passing through affection after affection

And yes, I am in love now-a-day

Never you came to me with love

Come before the last dawn of my life, I pray!

Hello, Buddy, How Are You?

(To Shah Abu Rushd Al Muneer)

Taking my hand in his and says, "See you again"

On a quiet evening, leaving

For the last time, he went far far away,

Gray to grayer, finally became a mere memory.

He dissolved in this city of memories

Among millions of people like a stream

But within my - myself he left

A solitary tremor of attachment

Among the crowd of thousands, every day

I have been looking for his face- the loving face

wherever I have been

I have sensed his secret presence.

Nobody else knows but I.

Not tears; not even the blood of the heart;

Just his presences

Awake my inert feeling.

Tears always fall from eyes,

Flowers fall from trees,

But memories never just fall.

However, I live like a prehistoric turtle

With ancient algae all over;

But even one more time

I am anxious about that touch;

Not a single word at all; not any song;

Even not a poetry;

But in the garden of catenary memories

I wish to keep my hand on his hand and tell him once

'Hello, buddy, how are you?'

I'm waiting for him to be quiet

For the day I can capture him alone

On our (remember?) packed, crowded, grayed street.

Maybe a day we will meet on the way;

He will tug my shirt behind;

Both eyes will look into mine with lots of wonders;

Hand to hand for a long span of time;

Neither any song;

Not even favorite poetry;

Just to spend sitting face to face.

He is still there in me,

And I have faith, he will return at some point.

Ignoring friendship,

No one can remain for long.

So, What the Name Should Be?

In the body with ripple, where do you go?

O the lady, nymph of eternal beauty!

O eternal young lady, your vibrating broad hips and raised breast

Generate a stream in the body

As well as a vortex,

But that wave does not rise in the heart!

Once the lady trembled my heart

In the sun-dappled golden noon of youth;

Her hot gaze burned my young heart;

Thirty-three years ago;

There was the flesh and blood;

There was an indescribable deep new vibration;

And there was the heat of love

Rooted in the body that burns deep in the heart!

However, the body has never burned like that before!

Now in this middle of age, why do I remember?

That the hidden burning resides

On the nipples and rises of the woman's juicy pair of breasts;

Hot lips and tongue;

And crotch and shank.

Its undetected influencer is passion.

There isn't any love, but it still burns.

The most intense, scorching wildfire is burning in the forest of the body!

Whether the physique is cuter than love to it!

Is it defeated by the body nowadays?

The aggressive fire of love!

In the desire to churn

The outcry in the sexual pleasure of the praying lady

Is awakened in the loveless body

Secretly lonesome midnight;

For sure I know it is not a love

So, what should the name be?

Are You Remaining the Same As Before Yet?

Aha! How long have not I seen you?

Your crystal-clear water is not touched

How long you do not soak me wet?

My heart lies on the softness of your chest.

Do yet as early days deep green trees

Does cast shadows on your dark, black eyes?

Does still at the pin-drop silence of the night rest

Do the moon play with its light on your chest?

Aha! So many days I do wait

To hear the source stream sound

From your chest?

Every minute I had counting in my mind

For such a long day

In your steaming water to be wet tumultuously

Moments have passed after moments.

Days have passed following days.

Now I am at the edge of my long careless swain days

The sky of my heart is downing with twilight

Still, my heart is in thirst only for you, why?

Why does thee awaken me every moment

To visit you again and again yet now!

Oh, my Shitalakshya

The first love of mine

Do you remain the same as before yet?

My Sweetheart, My Fantasy

In the glance of your eye

Once upon a time, all my days and nights

Fled away with!

Like the dew-dropping, pitter-patter sound

Your voice, I heard

And I woke up from my bed many days!

Even in my dreams, I could listen

Your laughter as the broken crystal bangle!

On a silent morning

Seeing dew-soaked red-rose bud

Many times

I thought it was your tears, by mistake!

And seeing the rain I thought

Your incessant crying!

What a huge oversight I had been imagining!

In fact, neither you ever not any day

Nowhere you were my sweet heart;

My fantasy!

My Demise and the Birth of a Love

Indeed that day

At that precious jiff, I had died;

Thirty years back;

On one of the golden-dreary summer noons;

Then the heat of her dazzling gaze

Burned in whole the body of my heart;

There was so much heat in that fire of sight;

That burnt me

And I became ashes inside;

At that fire as fierce as a wildfire

It burned to ashes that I had carefully nurtured

The verdant forest of mine;

Even then, from her eyes

I simply couldn't take my eyes off;

As though to be burnt off by that fire

Into this world I was born;

I was born

For such a fortunate death;

The death that was neither this world

Not any livings ever witnessed before.

Withered Leaves

Frost descends before the evening of the winter;

To their nest the birds flock back;

The sound of withered leaves covered by the flapping of wings;

The pitiful wail wakes up in the heart;

Life leaf has dried up slowly

In weariness and negligence;

In the cool breeze floats

The pitiful cry of withered leaves;

The days of life have fallen from the tree.

Beneath the sky in mild twilight

An alone passerby looks back today

And as if he is crying silently;

In a formless sense of pain;

In the darkness of the new moon, he might have been
perplexed;

A blind does not see the full moon;

With the pitter-patter sounds like dew

Melted silver - Moonlight is dripping;

He doesn't see, the landscape is swept away by the softness
of the light;

However, his heart becomes frozen;

However, only one desire remains yet:

Just a little warmth;

That the warmth of one-time

Burned every moment;

And poured honey

On his sharpened body;

Drove him around

On the ways of the world;

From within the country

Migrated him to another vibrant land;

Within the soft-tender arms of youth;

Within the folds of a woman's charming, graceful body;

Inside the orange's juicy, carpel-like lips;

Inside the fragrance of honeyed roses;

Today, there is no honey and no honeymoon.

None of the emotions—desire, rage, passion,

Or sound of delightful sensations—

They could not survive the passage of time.

One day because of love

Rose bloomed in his body and soul;

However, everything has fallen like stars;

It oozes off this winter afternoon.

The Song by a Youthful Heart

See, the woman awake on the pilgrimage of desire

Your woman is waiting to awaken for you

In the sleepless night of deep-frost-fog;

For so long, whom you have been love unknowingly.

When it rains a lot and it is sunny.

Rubicund butter-like fat in the waist

A desire arose in that body

The fire of desire burnt the green fantasy of youth

Then today truth will really become true!

Summer pain in every body today

Duel submission at the peak of warmth

Fount is wetted in frequent rains

Let then the imagination come true today!

As if the hidden agony in nipples

Is calling you, just you, today

Secretly in the sweet song;

Let then start singing, the song of youth,

Let it sung the warm body-music.

Even only the touch becomes the deep cry of youth today

The river of waiting is in the full monsoon now

The body becomes overflowing in lear by lear

Soft, sweet secret call of the silvergrass

In the white autumn of fulfillment.

The first bite of youth was in ruining prejudition

The body is also sacrosanct like a temple

The time of worship goes by

Come, my love; the first friend of life!

The Silence

Like the dusk following a twilight

Your pitiful silence

Sometimes suddenly

Becomes vocal in my yearning heart;

Dances like the golden sunlight on the green leaves;

Dances just in its own language;

Silence becomes quieter

Than silence;

And then secretly

Like the wings of a bird, it sounds

All our stories in strict secret.

And when you put your hands on my hand-

Your phenomenal and moonlight-like soft hand,

My whole affection is conveyed

In the calm, dark, soundless evening;

It gathers in my heart-

The sounds and vibrations emanating from your lofty
breasts;

Gradually the silence began to gain its voice;

Our ravenous body slowly awakens;

Like Rabindra Sangeet, I start singing and

The whole world sang together

The sacred physique song;

I understand that

Silence also speaks its own language

And creates its own song

When you keep a warm touch

On this thirsty beak of mine.

Taking up the life of silence in hand

Looking for your hands

A born blind, overwhelming, and wild man;

And silence in its fragrant water

Swept away by the sound of the whispering stream river.

$\mathscr{P}$rostration

The ultimate reality is the body

In this human life, No not love at all;

The craving for lust clothed in a label

That is called love

Love without sex is a mythical concept

What do men and women desire without lust?

Love without desire is like a stone sculpture

Neither only the lovers

Dating back thousands of years;

Not only in poetry or epics,

But you are the proof of this nowadays.

Whoever seeks a lady without beauty?

Beauty is held within the body.

For aesthetic,age after age

The world is at war, and blood is flowing;

History says the lover has left his kingdom

And migrated abroad

Think, where the beauty lies?

A lot of plants, rivers, and flowers in the environment

Birds are chirping all across our kind world.

Even my greatest love from the sea and the mountains,

My lady,

You are the soul of my existence;

Thank you! My prostration to you!

Insatiable Love

Did you forget

Once your heart was stagnantly frozen like a dead star

Who lit a warm fire there late at night one day?

Here, this is all your crimson-colored fruits

Juicy lips nowadays become gourmand-hungry fire;

There in the dark of the pupil of your eyes

Now, the wet monsoon flashed lightning;

Your body is like a teenage river

Terrible electric shocks in crooked alleyways;

At your weighty loin - that is shaped like an apple sliced in half,

Rash Brahmaputra's reckless,enamored wave there;

Your overbearing young breasts are Radiated

The strange attraction of smooth moonlight,

Hands are as delicate as the young creeper of the gourd

And the fragrance of the blooming rose is in your sight;

For a violent storm that screws up all

And for the drizzling rain

Your lonesome secret cry in the lonely late night;

Who did you keep it for?

Still, care so deeply?

If you really loved me

By weaving the life-giving seed of youth in the blood of the body;

The stubborn body never obeys any wall of border

And the body is the lotus of love!

But you yet awaiting

For a fabulous and colorful bridal bed;

And so,you're burning yourself out

In secret for a failure

Burning yourself inside in furious, burning flames;

You don't understand

Even the heart has its own body;

One can get it in love.

In the late afternoon's lovely, sorrowful light

As the shadows grow longer and lengthen

All of your days and nights are twilight today;

Yet you know not

In the blood of my love

Your pink heart lives,

And in each and every carves of your body

The golden sweat of my love is there;

But never you understand yet

The grandeur of our love;

If ever the sun never exists

Could the full moon rise in the sky?

Those Exposed Feet of Yours

Seemed all of a sudden, the beauty

Of the universe as a whole

Fell on its knees that day

To the pair of your exquisitely white, soft

and the exposed feet.

On a depressingly boring afternoon

I was stunned to see

Those exposed feet of yours - soft and smooth as butter.

From those of your feet

The silvery dispersion of the melting moonlight

At the moves of your shaped nails

And your silky, smooth skin;

It was only floating in my ears

A strange, gentle, melodious sound of the bejeweled
bracelet;

And I was gradually drifting away

In a secret deep hole in the moonlight

I was floating

In an unsaid sensation of a lustful obsession;

I grew extremely thirsty and impatient

Of those brocade-like feet of yours

To touch just a bit

Since it was those feet that roused my

Slumber flames of dormant youth;

Likes usually begin with the feet.

Finally, there are footsteps;

But you don't know

A barefoot woman in adolescence

Showing her hidden beauty

While blinding me with the arrows of merciless cruelty

Before stealthily escaping.

Long have I sought her in solitary secrecy

Like a cool sunset

She disappeared into an unfamiliar darkness

But she lit the first fire on my body

I seek her secretly

Beyond the boundary of this wide field

On the golden edge of youth;

I have been looking for a long

That inebriating fragrance of her

Sweaty folds of the arms,

That the woman lost

Like a colorless drop of sweating

Adorned in classical ornaments.

These blazing feet of yours

Will destroy cities, towns, and ports

The men's eager hearts are awake and waiting;

Do men know in those lovely, tender feet

There is fire's strength?Not the flame of beauty burned herself?

Only burns in its combustion

Man's life and youth!

But even yet there in my eyes

The dreams spread their wings slowly

And one after one

I keep kissing, the warmth

Those beautiful bare feet are like a sculpture;

And immediately one by one

There began to emerge

Thousands of red Iranian roses!

The Fire-Spark of Youth

About that fire spark that was suddenly burned

I could not forget even today;

But today I can understand

I was also burned that day

In the high conflagration that belongs to youth;

Even though I was aware of the pain of burning

Even then I did not understand the delight to burn others.

The volcano that was dormant inside me

Its crater was so calm and quiet

Before touching you;

I was buried inside there

As ancient pharaohs are still buried today

In the secret chambers of the pyramids;

Even slightest touch of yours

Made me so horrible and destructive that time

Fiery lava of the early youth

Continued to be flung forth throughout the day

And burned in and burned out to ashes

All the villages and cities and ports of my body

I was in such pain then

And you took me out

From the burning ash of the lava

Raises again

Resurrected like a phoenix!

Since then, I have feels only

Itburns and burns

Burning and only burning

Silently for hundreds of thousands of years;

There is no end to this scorch

There is no end to this smolder

What the kind of seeds have you sown

That is deathless life, within me!

I wanted to be asleep

Eternity;

In the ways, on a winter night,

Young men - women sleep after making love;

Just like a mountain or an ancient river does.

You silently broke the lonesome solitude

And woke me up one day

And raised all the prehistoric cities and towns within my
body

But you don't reside in that city

You don't have a house in that village

Not all places are drenched with moonlight.

Your affection turned into a cold stone.

I'm trapped underneath,

Thus,I'm unable to sleep.

And yet I am just

Looking for you, even after being burned,

In village after village; city after city;

Only seeking for you

And in the fire of omnivorous youth

I also was burnt to ashes at one time;

But I again rose from the ashes like a phoenix

In the fairy tale of life!

The Aroma of Passion

Nevertheless, one day I will hug her tight

Whom I have lost of neglect in every moment

Who was loving me in her teenage

As the smell of a new harvest

On a crazy evening

She wanted to be primitive in love

In lonely darkness, with lips on lips

I had refused her repeatedly,

Despite the terrible sorrow of a young heart torn

She is my love - my first love.

But she continued to come back.

At the threshold of my awareness,

In the drowsy sensibility of my sleep

She grew up as fast as a fast-growing plant do

Comes back with a strange moonlight on the top of her
palm,

And then the new moon desires to devour

My sleepless, lifeless, parched heart.

All the painful memories

Turn into a river and flows inside the eyes,

She walks along the earthen ridge of the green field

With her soft, fluffy body like a rabbit

And with my broken love

I can't sleep longer anymore.

Daily, amid the increasing power of separation

Burned herself alone inside

Her dusty, cold, dream-world was afflicted

She is not, however, angry or depressed.

No difficulty in not getting

What an untold love was given to her

In cruel illusions deceptively

Alone she lighted up in the moonless sky

A lamp of soft moonlight

Inside the bamboo grove,

Beside the faint dusty path of the forest

She has decorated the temple of her tender love

Neither evening prayer, no lamps of worship today

Yet she mingles in darkness

With a strange desire

Maybe one day, dawn really does rise

On one morning

When familiar teen footsteps are heard

She will awaken once again.

There will be an end to the very long wait.

Life will emerge at some point.

In a passionate hug of affection,

Life with verbosity will reawaken all around once again.

Rain will float her chest again.

She eventually set her desire back aside.

And falls asleep soundly.

On a winter's warm noon

I still awaken to the sound of a dove cooing.

Still, she awakens at my side like a shadow,

Watching over me day or night.

That fragrance doesn't come from flesh;

That's the intense love of a woman,

For that the smell yet I am living,

With the manliness of my virgin heart!

Do You Feel, Sweetheart?

Only she is remembered

Why is only she remembered today?

On this dark evening of a monsoon

In the soaking wet, drunken breeze

As memories flood in, my mind becomes soggy.

So many words I could recall.

So many words come to mind.

On such a lonely dark evening

Just you and me

We got lost away one day

Far away in the unknown - beyond our knowledge

In a depressing sorrow for the mental obsession with love

And again, we came back too

Along parallel railway lines

Drenched in unceasing rain

By holding each other's hands;

In the sudden touch of your wet breasts

I understood how slowly

Each rose blossoms from the bud

How to say a lot without talking

In the invisible thread of love

How to bond together without touching

Two innocent hearts!

But I didn't understand then

A heart can be pledged to another heart

But the body does not go

One day the body leaves

It leaves a sharp pain

Throughout life

Left the skeleton of love!

From then until now

Till thirty-three years

On every evening of the rainy August

And on every stormy night

I can feel the warm touch of your breath

In the deepest of my sensation

But you are not there

Neither the aroma of your lovely body;

Not a lonely night so long and

So dark as your hair.

Floating on flood water comes to the ears

The crying sound of separation

I float and floated further

On each silver-colored, full-moon night

Then also the world is floated away

In the surprising full flood of the moonlight

It rained across my sky

Drops of pain fall drop after drops

Each day and each night

Seems so long to me

The tired heart is ruminated by memories

Blood oozed

And only the blood oozes deep into the heart

The warm flow of blood is a flowing river now

There is the sad sound of the river streams

Could you hear that

Sweetheart?

Sex and the Mask

Sex, as you think

Untold should stay

Show silence and

Attachment nay

An attachment to sex

Does anyone want to bridle?

One covers the face in Silence

Afraid of shame moves sidle!

Eternal truthis sex

Not ever to strife

Hoping for love and mating

Remains throughout life.

Sex means only

Obscenity, no not that

From the primitive until now

Sex wins, not to jest at

Cultivation of sex

Creates humans

Without sex

World, not happen

First Meeting

Eagerly I was waiting then

For your warm touch just once

The sound of your footstep unseen

My heart keeps beating endlessly

I was so excited that my body was quivering,

Yet I was waiting for you;

The sky's sunlight

Gradually turns yellow to orange;

And my misery of waiting just becomes worse

You suddenly emerged in grandeur.

On your lotus-petal-like feet,

The anklet is jingling when you walk.

Its rhythm was matched by the pace of my heart.

In the unskillful hands of the first youth

You were worn with a great care

Red, black striped saree.

Soft and puffy like white butter

The visible part of your physique,

Soft tender areas of your body,

Your heavy hips and breasts;

And fling in the air

Your long black hair

As if all of a sudden, my-

Heart stopped all the beating

I couldn't look you in the eyes.

That was the first time in my life

I lost consciousness!

I had a great longing that, one day

I will touch and see you,

I will touch one day,

All the tender fingers of your hand;

We will bathe in the sea.

In the deep, black forest of your eyes

One day I was lost

I thought while looking for you

It would be better to be lost

Why is it necessary to be thirsty to win your heart?

But I was unable to get back by myself!

I looked for you a few times and finally

I backed again and again to the same heart line.

Never Came Before

Such a gorgeous night

Never came into my life before.

Up till the horizon, the moon's glittering light drifted.

There is quietness around,

And you have taken all over my universe.

As soon as I touch your finger my body's electricity flashed

I became drowsy with a wounded body

I drift slowly - drifted

I have flowed away from the Meghna into the gray estuary
of the far Brahmaputra

I Float from one sea to another ocean

Placed you as a center and I whirl around you

From one world to the dark bluish of another world

As if I keep floating life after life

In the lukewarm warmth of your love.

Night after night and even super night passed

I slowly wake up from that slumber

And from within the deep sleep

I Wake up and seek a shelter

At Your soft silky body;

As if a little warmth was my absolute need

From thousands of light years ago;

I am looking for warmth

I just keep searching like a cat.

I touched your fingers one after another

And slowly I got warmer;

At your warm lips

I continue to draw kisses of love one after another;

Your two breasts were as soft as the full moon

Weretransports to me back to a dream world

I drifted off again;

I feel like I'm about to die

As your smooth navel gets closer

As if I am going to die

And I reach to your hidden world;

And I found   my own self;

I dissolved and drowned in your deep love.

The Song of Physique

In your eyes, drawn by kajal

The day my eyes fell for the first time

Everything in the world for a moment

Abruptly stopped that day

The heat of your dazzling gaze

Was spread in my body

And to the streets and lanes of its cities and ports

And was carried in every string of the heart

The thrill of love

Love all over the body

Trembling at the tinge of the melody

I could realize

Something is going to happen today

I could feel

Some ruining may be about to happen!

The touch of the sweet breeze of your flying veil

Paralyzing me all over the body

Love song started

Like falling leaves in the wind of the summer

And you took me away

To your lonely secret garden

Nobody else was there.

On that lovely summer afternoon

There was never anyone else

And there never will be

Except for you and me.

Your hair blowing in the wind

Its soft touch and smell

Makes me as drunk

Trembling of your proud breasts

Was announcing

Your unstained reckless youth

As I take a breath

I went crazy

My anxietyto touch you

Made me primitive

And took to the pinnacle of manhood;

I was dying again and again;

And the whole world then

Was quaking

In my every foot-step

That thrill of your first touch

Still keeps me awake;

It still shakes me

At the door of my sleepless night;

Love still calls me.

Fourteen Years Later

(To Shamina Chowdhury Shampa)

I finally saw you today after a long fourteen years

Like an ancient star

Whose blazing light extended into my heart,

Melted me like a candle, drop by drop

Within myself

Like melting silver, then

Gradually, I became stronger

And got shape again - a new shape

As though by a bored sculptor

I was just created.

I was startled

My heart was broken down

In clinking sound

The way your voice

Sounds like the breaking of a glass bangle

Since nineteen hundred eighty-four

On a gloomy afternoon of a cloudy day

Then it disappeared

Slowly in deeper darkness.

I loved you and you - from head to toe

I loved you as in a secluded forest

Living a monk

No one else in the world

Ever loved anybody like this

No one else could float you

As I can float you in love

In the water of passionate love

The way I did love you

Loved you beneath an orange light

On a fragranced afternoon

Loved beyond all my desire-rage

Then I became a monk

More than a monk.

I got swept away

Much like the dried leaves floating in the breeze

I had been carried away on that serene summer afternoon.

I was aware that

One day I will have to sacrifice everything for love

All that I have

Even all I could have in the future

But I keep coming back

To the fire like a moth

I went up in ashes

Awaken once again

Such as a phoenix

Consciously or subconsciously

My love continually awakens with me

I rediscover love

I know that love has robbed me

And love made me fulfilled but even empty too.

Every second of every day, I fall more and more in love

If only for one more time, with love

I can blossom flowers on stones.

I would bet everything on love

And desire to float me and floated

Both the side of my heart.

The Kisses: Not Done Yet

I wish I died again and again

And wishes to be born again and again in this green Bengal

I want to be mixed in the wildness of vines

and with the shy split leaves of the Mimosa pudica plants

I want to get wet in monsoon rain every now and then

Just you and me

Beneath the umbrella of the teak green

Or I can watch while getting drenched in the November
fog.

How the golden dew is swallowed by the rising sun!

I wish to immerse in space

Beneath the shadow of autumn's white clouds;

Blended in the aroma of winter's paddy field

The brisk breeze floating;

Get mixed up with the poor farmer's

Glowing pious grin

And that I might live forever

In the wonderful shade of nature and trees

Otherwise, in this quiet intensive

Water of this pond I float, I willed

Beyond the hope of life.

Let me swim underwater

In this crystal-clear water of the waterbody that smelled of
lotus

Let's mingle with the blossoms of water-lily and
water-hyacinth.

I enjoy going.

At my personal river of mine

And feel Shitalakshya's refreshing stream of water

Additionally, let's speak at the ferry dock.

The beaming boatman.

Once again, I wish to visit

My cherished adolescent years.

To that erratic girl,

With whom I have deposited

All my teen's secrets

And all of my growing-up hardships;

In whose eyes I once saw the green forest.

Whose lips may still be holding my

Warm and moist kisses:

Not done yet!

Expectations of the Generation

On the journey to this filthy world,

I shall leave a trace of my footsteps

And there always be my exalted head

Let the honesty would the new heps

The germs of bravery and justice

Revolting against the betrayal of freedom

Fire in blood in blazing protest

Impotent creatures do depart, no need 'em.

Plato, Crito, and Socrates

Still here in the mind

Why in the world so much mess?

It seems no life in humankind

The knowledge flames will chase darkness

The ongoing strange circus of ignorant fools

The new generation will no longer accept it

At the blue sky of their expectation rules.

At Twilight

In love a picture with colors I draw

This twilight it has been torn in raw

Yet I sit with brush in hand to saw

Life has no color but darkness has claw.

Many words, many memories I do remember now

On my eyes thesteamed raining is thou

The stream of blood from my heart makes everything bow

Why the weary traveler looks back and raises an eyebrow?

For the price of life, I bought the ferocious inferno of pain

Why does love burns me today, what is the desire of the brain?

If all were to end one day, alas why not now, today then?

Oh god, you gave me everything, I do pray, alone I am in vain.

Towards Sunset

Each dawn is unique.

The usual very known mornings

Changes into different looks

Golden rays were hidden by the fog

Gradually the cold increases

The pain in the heart became worse;

A dust storm of melancholy comes to the barren heart

Yet it is unable to expel

The sorrow, agony, and grief of the people

The poor people onthis too-old planet

Being stricken with grief or sorrowNow it has become a stone

Fading into a life of gray and gloom

As though the curse of God had descended

Upon this Earth right now

Life does not, however, end.

There is constant weeping and misery.

Prostitution is becoming a greater sin;

But the world moves forth

Only towards the sunset.

The Adventure

Smoothly the evening falls

In the twilight of life

Calculation of demand and supply

All vanishes in the dark

Life leaves its mark

In this strange world;

All that I have acquired and desired.

One day, on the dot, I shall go from everything

The process will then resume.

A new deathless everlasting life

Thus, everything fell behind

The cycle of birth to death,

The loving life.

O my future, ever-unknown

Let the adventure begin!

Considering the Last Day

One day, I won't be awake.

On the clear, holy morning

I won't go up to the balcony to see the flowers bloomed

The Bougainvillea continued to be absorbed.

Will cast its charm across the dawning sky.

Madhavilata took a grip

Of the grill on the balcony, maybe,

The sunrise still twirls its golden light

Across the green leaves

The creeper of Aparajita may have stretched

Her blooming green finger

In the utmost ecstasy of existence.

The torrential rain of the previous night

May have given them

A blossom of new life

But I won't stay anymore

Since I regularly reside in this room

And pay them a visit on the balcony

I am at the end of the trip

My life on this side

Will finally end everything

As I run out of cigarettes every day;

However, whether in the morning?

That little tailor bird will search me

Out of curiosity or

in Immense love!

In the flood of moonlight while the Sahari ends

After praying at Fajr

On the verge of endless sleepless exhaustion

In a soft feather white bed

Lying down next to my beloved wife in a deep sleep

Will she know?

I will leave today!

Perhaps not anymore

Together, we'll see the rainy night

The moon of moonlit night in solitude and silence

We won't ever again drink tea late at night.

The story, the poetry, the song beneath the shade of
moonlight

A wonderful illusion lights the darkness

I might be unable to hold again

Her soft magical hands!

If she implied that I had died,

The eyesight is moribund, and the feculent eyes are closing.

Can she still survive?

Will she succeed?

The immeasurable waves of life;

If she has no one by her side,

And really no one with love.

A melodic death cry comparable to the call to prayer

Is anyone able to ignore it?

One Day, I Might Be Murdered

I know

One day, I might be murdered

Crossfires could result in deaths

Or an assassination.

It may be so

Using the state machinery to hang me

The death penalty may be imposed

My apprehension is that I am open to public gatherings

Beheading can also be done with a shiny, sharp sword

And that will be the demand of modernity at that time

Because our nation is now gradually entering

The complex reactionary plot

As though some virus-infected people

Don't even know they are harboring the virus

And unknowingly passing it from one body to another.

In this manner, the virus of a communal conspiracy is spreading,

The virus of religious malice, reactivity virus

For centuries after eons, over the years'

In the holy crime of preventing this dreaded virus infection

I may be killed, at any time.

In the interest of human security, I might be murdered,

I might be put to death for the sake of civilization's security,

In the sake of religious security, I might be murdered.

I might even be killed

In the cause of defending the truth.

This modern, venomed civilization

Killing can also be done in the name of its protection

Because I could pose

A serious threat to them all in the future

They feared that even with dangerous weapons at their
disposal,

They might as well kill me to protect themselves.

One day, there may be 7.5 billion people who are aware.

What an utterly defenseless man!

A state armed with deadly weapons can pose a threat

And against his blind followers

I'll be killed because of them

I convey justice and accuracy.

I discuss morals and values;

I speak of morals and ideals,

Of Socrates, Rabindranath,

And of the hopes of people.

Discuss releasing individuals from slavery

I am a man who possesses the most terrifying weapon in
existence,

And nearly everyone in this world is terrified of me

They will thus kill me and

Eradicate me from this earth

But they are clueless.

Even when there are deaths,

Truth and principles endure.